vodka

vodka

invigorating vodka cocktails

Bath · New York · Singapore · Hong Kong · Cologne · Delhi · Melbourne

First published by Parragon in 2007

Parragon
Queen Street House
4 Queen Street
Bath BA1 1HE

Designed by Talking Design
Photography by Mike Cooper
Introduction text and additional recipes by Linda Doeser
Food Styling by Lincoln Jefferson and Carole Handslip

ISBN 978-1-4054-9509-7

Printed in China

WARNING

Recipes containing raw eggs are not suitable for convalescents, the
elderly or pregnant women. Please consume alcohol responsibly.

CONTENTS

introduction

Vodka is versatile, combining well with lots of mixers and juices, and the introduction of flavoured vodkas has vastly increased the repertoire of contemporary cocktails. Making cocktails isn't difficult and is great fun. Reading the following guidelines should ensure you have all the skills of a professional bartender at your fingertips.

Measures

Measuring the quantities is one of the keys to making a good cocktail. The standard single measure is 25 ml/1 fl oz, as used throughout this book. You can decide to use your own standard measure as long as you follow the proportions given in the recipes.

Bar Essentials

Cocktail shaker The standard type is a cylindrical 500-ml/ 18-fl oz container with a double lid incorporating a strainer. The Boston shaker consists of double conical containers without a strainer.

Mixing glass You can use the container of your cocktail shaker, a jug about the same size or a professional mixing glass.

Strainer A bar strainer prevents ice from being poured into the serving glass. You could also use a small nylon sieve.

Jigger This small measuring cup is often double-ended. Standard jiggers are 25 ml/1 fl oz and 35 ml/1½ fl oz, representing 1 and 1½ measures respectively. If you don't have a jigger, use a liqueur, schnapps or shot glass.

Bar spoon This long-handled spoon is used for stirring cocktails in a mixing glass.

Other basics Lots of kitchen equipment is useful: corkscrew, cocktail sticks, citrus juicer,

chopping board, kitchen knives, citrus zester and a blender. You will require an ice bucket and tongs.

Glasses

Cocktail/Martini glass
Stemmed glass with a cone-shaped bowl (125–150 ml/4–5 fl oz)

Highball glass Tall straight glass (225 ml/8 fl oz)

Collins glass Tall narrow glass with straight sides (300 ml/10 fl oz)

Shot glass Small glass (50 ml/2 fl oz)

Bartender's Tips

Shaking cocktails Remove the lid from the shaker, add ice and pour in the ingredients. Close and shake vigorously for 10–20 seconds, until the outside of the shaker is misty. Remove the small lid and pour the cocktail into the glass. If your shaker doesn't have an integral strainer,

use a separate one.

Stirring cocktails Put ice into a mixing glass, pour in the ingredients and stir vigorously for 20 seconds. Strain into a glass.

Sugar syrup Professionals use sugar syrup to sweeten cocktails. Put 4 tbsp caster sugar and 4 tbsp water into a saucepan. Gradually bring to the boil, stirring. Boil, without stirring, for 1–2 minutes, remove from the heat and leave to cool. Store in a sterilized bottle in the refrigerator for up to 2 months.

Chilling glasses Place glasses in the refrigerator for 2 hours before using. Alternatively, fill them with cracked ice, stir well, then tip out the ice before pouring in the cocktail.

Ice To crack ice, put cubes in a strong plastic bag and hit with the smooth side of a meat mallet or a rolling pin. Alternatively, bang the bag against a wall.

Renaissance

Cosmopolitan

INVITING AND REFRESHING, THE COSMOPOLITAN IS THE BEVERAGE
OF CHOICE FOR THE 'SEX AND THE CITY' GIRLS AND IS A MUST AT ANY
FASHIONABLE PARTY.'

SERVES 1
2 measures vodka
1 measure Triple Sec
1 measure fresh lime juice
1 measure cranberry juice
ice
orange peel, to decorate

1 Shake all the liquid
   ingredients over ice
   until well frosted.
2 Strain into a chilled
   cocktail glass.
3 Dress with a strip of
   orange peel.

Sex On The Beach

HOLIDAY DRINKS ARE OFTEN LONG AND FRUITY AND THIS REFRESHING
COCKTAIL IS REMINISCENT OF HAPPY DAYS IN THE SUN.

SERVES 1
1 measure peach schnapps
1 measure vodka
2 measures fresh orange juice
3 measures cranberry and
  peach juice
ice and crushed ice
dash of lemon juice
piece of orange peel, to
  decorate

1 Shake the first four
  ingredients over ice
  until well frosted.
2 Strain into a glass filled
  with crushed iced and
  squeeze on the lemon
  juice.
3 Dress with orange
  peel.

Japanese Slipper

JAPANESE BECAUSE MIDORI, THE BEST-KNOWN MELON LIQUEUR, IS MADE IN JAPAN AND SLIPPER, PRESUMABLY, BECAUSE IT'S SO EASY TO SWALLOW, NOT BECAUSE IT MAKES YOU SLIDE OVER.

SERVES 1
cracked ice
1½ measures vodka
1½ measures Midori
1 measure freshly squeezed
  lime juice
lime slice, to decorate
  (optional)

1 Put the cracked ice into a cocktail shaker and pour in the vodka, Midori and lime juice.
2 Cover and shake vigorously for 10–20 seconds, until the outside of the shaker is misted.
3 Strain into a cocktail glass and decorate with a lime slice, if you like.

Harvey Wallbanger

THIS WELL-KNOWN CONTEMPORARY CLASSIC COCKTAIL IS A GREAT PARTY DRINK – MIX IT STRONG AT FIRST, THEN WEAKER AS THE EVENING GOES BY – OR WITHOUT ALCOHOL FOR DRIVERS AND NO ONE WOULD KNOW...!

SERVES 1
ice cubes
3 measures vodka
8 measures orange juice
2 tsp Galliano
cherry and slice of orange,
  to decorate

1 Half fill a glass with ice, pour vodka and orange over the ice cubes, and float Galliano on top.

2 Garnish with a cherry and slice of orange.

3 For a warming variant, mix a splash of ginger wine with the vodka and orange.

Bloody Mary

THIS CLASSIC COCKTAIL WAS INVENTED IN 1921 AT THE LEGENDARY HARRY'S BAR IN PARIS. THERE ARE NUMEROUS VERSIONS – SOME MUCH HOTTER AND SPICIER. INGREDIENTS MAY INCLUDE HORSERADISH SAUCE IN ADDITION TO OR INSTEAD OF TABASCO SAUCE.

SERVES 1

dash of Worcestershire sauce
dash of Tabasco sauce
cracked ice cubes
2 measures vodka
splash of dry sherry
6 measures tomato juice
juice of ½ lemon
pinch of celery salt
pinch of cayenne pepper
celery stick with leaves
slice of lemon, to decorate

1 Dash the Worcestershire sauce and Tabasco sauce over ice in a shaker and add the vodka, splash of dry sherry, tomato juice and lemon juice.

2 Shake vigorously until frosted.

3 Strain into a tall chilled glass, add a pinch of celery salt and a pinch of cayenne and decorate with a celery stick and a slice of lemon.

Mudslide

DESPITE ITS OMINOUS–SOUNDING NAME, THIS IS A RICHLY FLAVOURED
CREAMY CONCOCTION THAT IS DELICIOUS WHATEVER THE WEATHER.

SERVES 1
1½ measures Kahlúa
1½ measures Baileys Irish
  Cream
1½ measures vodka
cracked ice cubes

1 Shake the Kahlúa,
  Baileys Irish Cream and
  vodka vigorously over
  ice until well frosted.
2 Strain into a chilled
  glass.

Screwdriver

ALWAYS USE FRESHLY SQUEEZED ORANGE JUICE TO MAKE THIS
REFRESHING COCKTAIL – IT IS JUST NOT THE SAME WITH BOTTLED
JUICE. THIS SIMPLE, CLASSIC COCKTAIL HAS GIVEN RISE TO NUMEROUS
AND INCREASINGLY ELABORATE VARIATIONS.

SERVES 1
cracked ice cubes
2 measures vodka
orange juice
slice of orange, to decorate

1 Fill a chilled glass with
  cracked ice cubes.
2 Pour the vodka over
  the ice and top up with
  orange juice.
3 Stir well to mix and
  dress with a slice of
  orange.

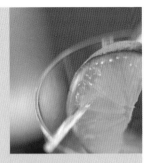

Long Island Iced Tea

DATING BACK TO THE DAYS OF THE AMERICAN PROHIBITION WHEN IT WAS DRUNK OUT OF CUPS IN AN ATTEMPT TO FOOL THE FBI THAT IT WAS HARMLESS, THIS COCKTAIL HAS EVOLVED FROM THE ORIGINAL SIMPLE COMBINATION OF VODKA WITH A DASH OF COLA!

SERVES 1

2 measures vodka
1 measure gin
1 measure white tequila
1 measure white rum
½ measure white crème de menthe
2 measures lemon juice
1 tsp sugar syrup
cracked ice cubes
cola
wedge of lime or lemon, to decorate

1 Shake the vodka, gin, tequila, rum, crème de menthe, lemon juice and sugar syrup vigorously over ice until well frosted.
2 Strain into an ice-filled glass and top up with cola.
3 Dress with lime or lemon wedges.

Seabreeze

PINK GRAPEFRUIT JUICE IS MUCH SWEETER AND SUBTLER THAN ITS
PALER COUSIN, SO IT IS IDEAL TO MIX IN COCKTAILS WHERE YOU WANT
JUST A SLIGHT SHARPNESS.

SERVES 1
1½ measures vodka
½ measure cranberry juice
ice
pink grapefruit juice to taste

1 Shake the vodka and
cranberry juice over ice
until frosted.
2 Pour into a chilled
tumbler or long glass
and top up with pink
grapefruit juice to
taste.
3 Serve with a straw.

Blue Lagoon

LET YOUR IMAGINATION CARRY YOU AWAY WHILE YOU SINK INTO THIS
LUXURIOUSLY BLUE COCKTAIL. IT HAS A REFRESHING LEMON ZING AND
SPARKLE TOO.

SERVES 1
1 measure blue Curaçao
1 measure vodka
dash of fresh lemon juice
lemonade

1 Pour the blue Curaçao
into a highball or
cocktail glass, followed
by the vodka.
2 Add the lemon juice
and top up with
lemonade to taste.

Black Russian

HISTORY RECORDS ONLY WHITE AND RED RUSSIANS. THE OMISSION OF THE BLACK RUSSIAN IS A SAD OVERSIGHT. FOR A COFFEE LIQUEUR, YOU CAN USE EITHER TIA MARIA OR KAHLÚA, DEPENDING ON YOUR PERSONAL TASTE – THE LATTER IS SWEETER.

SERVES 1
2 measures vodka
1 measure coffee liqueur
4–6 cracked ice cubes

1 Pour the vodka and liqueur over cracked ice cubes in a small chilled glass.
2 Stir to mix.

Anouchka

SAMBUCA IS LIQUORICE FLAVOURED AND THEREFORE NOT
TO EVERYONE'S TASTE. HOWEVER, USED HERE WITH A DASH
OF BLACKBERRY LIQUEUR AND THE ICED VODKA, IT'S A GREAT
COMBINATION.

SERVES 1
1 measure vodka, iced
dash black Sambuca
dash crème de mure
a few blackberries, to
  decorate

1 Pour the vodka into a
  chilled shot glass.
2 Add a dash of
  Sambuca and then
  a dash of crème de
  mure.
3 Dress with a few
  blackberries, fresh or
  frozen.

Russian Double

VODKA AND SCHNAPPS ARE BOTH VERY STRONG DRINKS, SO HANDLE WITH CARE!

SERVES 1
1 measure vodka, iced
strips of lemon or orange
   peel
1 measure lemon vodka or
   schnapps, iced

1 Layer the drinks
carefully in a chilled
shot glass, putting a
piece of peel in the
first layer and drink
immediately.

Godmother

AMARETTO IS AN ITALIAN LIQUEUR, SO PERHAPS THE INSPIRATION FOR THIS COCKTAIL COMES FROM DON CORLEONE, THE PROTAGONIST IN MARIO PUZO'S BEST-SELLING NOVEL, UNFORGETTABLY PORTRAYED IN THE FILM BY MARLON BRANDO.

SERVES 1
cracked ice cubes
2 measures vodka
1 measure Amaretto

1 Put 4–6 cracked ice cubes into a small chilled tumbler.
2 Pour 2 measures vodka and 1 measure Amaretto over the ice. Shake to mix.

Innovative

Woo-woo

BE SURE TO WOO YOUR FRIENDS WITH THIS REFRESHING AND SIMPLE
DRINK. IT'S ALSO GREAT FOR PARTIES.

SERVES 1
cracked ice cubes
2 measures vodka
2 measures peach schnapps
4 measures cranberry juice
physalis (cape gooseberry), to
 decorate

1 Half fill a chilled
 cocktail glass with
 cracked ice.
2 Pour the vodka,
 peach schnapps and
 cranberry juice over
 the ice.
3 Stir well to mix and
 decorate with a
 physalis.

Moscow Mule

THIS COCKTAIL CAME INTO EXISTENCE THROUGH A HAPPY
COINCIDENCE DURING THE 1930S. AN AMERICAN BAR OWNER HAD
OVERSTOCKED GINGER BEER AND A REPRESENTATIVE OF A SOFT
DRINKS COMPANY INVENTED THE MOSCOW MULE TO HELP HIM OUT.

SERVES 1
2 measures vodka
1 measure lime juice
cracked ice cubes
ginger beer
slice of lime, to decorate

1 Shake the vodka and lime juice vigorously over ice until well frosted.

2 Half fill a chilled glass with cracked ice cubes and strain the cocktail over them.

3 Top up with ginger beer. Dress with a slice of lime.

Fuzzy Navel

THIS IS ANOTHER ONE OF THOSE COCKTAILS WITH A NAME THAT PLAYS
ON THE INGREDIENTS – FUZZY TO REMIND YOU THAT IT CONTAINS
PEACH SCHNAPPS AND NAVEL BECAUSE IT IS MIXED WITH ORANGE
JUICE.

SERVES 1
2 measures vodka
1 measure peach schnapps
8 fl oz/250 ml orange juice
cracked ice cubes
physalis (cape gooseberry),
    to decorate

1 Shake the vodka,
   peach schnapps and
   orange juice vigorously
   over cracked ice until
   well frosted.
2 Strain into a chilled
   cocktail glass and
   decorate with a
   physalis.

Strawberrini

WONDERFULLY FRESH TASTING WITH A SMELL OF SUMMER THAT WILL TAKE AWAY ALL YOUR CARES...

SERVES 1
1 oz/30 g fresh or frozen strawberries
1 tbsp caster sugar
1–2 drops fresh lime juice
splash of fraise
2 measures vodka, well iced

1 Reserve 2–3 strawberries to add later.
2 Crush the rest in a bowl with the sugar, lime juice and fraise.
3 Strain well.
4 Pour the vodka into an iced cocktail glass and add the purée and reserved strawberries.

Salty Dog

WHEN THIS COCKTAIL FIRST APPEARED, GIN-BASED MIXES WERE BY FAR THE MOST POPULAR, BUT NOWADAYS, A SALTY DOG IS MORE FREQUENTLY MADE WITH VODKA. CHOOSE WHICHEVER YOU PREFER, BUT THE COCKTAILS WILL HAVE DIFFERENT FLAVOURS.

SERVES 1
1 tbsp granulated sugar
1 tbsp coarse salt
lemon half
6–8 cracked ice cubes
2 measures vodka
grapefruit juice

1 Mix the sugar and salt in a saucer. Rub the rim of a chilled glass with the lemon half, then dip it in the sugar and salt mixture to frost.

2 Fill the glass with cracked ice cubes and pour the vodka over them.

3 Top up with grapefruit juice and stir to mix. Drink with a straw.

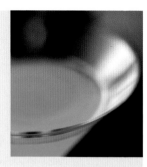

Blue Monday

THE LOVELY COLOUR AND FRUITY FLAVOUR OF THIS COCKTAIL ARE
GUARANTEED TO MAKE MONDAY YOUR FAVOURITE DAY OF THE WEEK.

SERVES 1
cracked ice
1 measure vodka
½ measure Cointreau
1 tbsp blue Curaçao

1 Put the cracked ice
into a mixing glass or
jug and pour in the
vodka, Cointreau and
Curaçao. Stir well and
strain into a cocktail
glass.

Bellinitini

THIS IS A VARIATION ON THE CLASSIC BELLINI COCKTAIL. A GREAT WAY TO USE UP YOUR LEFT OVER NEW YEAR'S EVE BUBBLY – ALTHOUGH YOU COULD ALSO USE PROSECCO OR SPARKLING WINE.

SERVES 1
2 measures vodka
1 measure peach schnapps
1 measure peach juice
chilled champagne

1 Shake the vodka, peach schnapps and peach juice vigorously until well frosted.
2 Strain into a chilled champagne flute.
3 Top up with chilled champagne.

Seeing Red

THERE IS A REAL KICK TO THIS COCKTAIL AND THE VIVID COLOUR
COMES FROM THE CRANBERRY JUICE.

SERVES 1
1 measure red vodka
1 measure peach schnapps
3 measures cranberry juice
crushed ice
soda water
frozen cranberries, to
   decorate

1 Shake the first three
   ingredients over
   crushed ice until well
   frosted.
2 Strain into a tall chilled
   glass, top up with soda
   water and float a few
   frozen cranberries on
   the top.

Raspberrini

FRESH AND FRUITY, THIS COCKTAIL IS PERFECT FOR THOSE BALMY
SUMMER EVENINGS.

SERVES 1
1 oz/30 g fresh or frozen
    raspberries
1 tbsp caster sugar
1–2 drops fresh lemon juice
splash of framboise
2 measures vodka, well iced

1 Reserve 2–3 raspberries
   to add later.
2 Crush the rest in a
   bowl with the sugar,
   lemon and framboise.
3 Strain well.
4 Pour the vodka into an
   iced glass and add the
   purée and reserved
   raspberries.

Spotted Bikini

A CHEEKY NAME FOR AN AMUSING COCKTAIL. IT ALSO TASTES GREAT,
ALTHOUGH YOU MAY LIKE TO ADD A LITTLE SUGAR TO TASTE.

SERVES 1
2 measures vodka
1 measure white rum
1 measure cold milk
juice ½ lemon
ice
1 ripe passion fruit
piece of lemon, to decorate

1 Shake the first four
   ingredients over ice
   until well frosted.
2 Strain into a chilled
   medium cocktail glass
   and add the passion
   fruit, not strained, at
   the last minute so you
   see the black seeds.
3 Dress with a piece of
   lemon.

Peartini

WHILE LESS POPULAR THAN PEACH OR CHERRY EAU DE VIE, PEAR BRANDY HAS A DELICATE FRAGRANCE AND LOVELY FLAVOUR, BUT DON'T CONFUSE IT WITH PEAR LIQUEUR.

SERVES 1
1 tsp caster sugar
pinch of ground cinnamon
1 lemon wedge
cracked ice
1 measure vodka
1 measure pear brandy, such as Poire William or Pera Segnana

1 Mix together the sugar and cinnamon on a saucer. Rub the outside rim of a cocktail glass with the lemon wedge, then dip it into the sugar and cinnamon mixture. Set aside.

2 Put the cracked ice into a mixing glass or jug and pour in the vodka and pear brandy. Stir well and strain into the prepared glass, without disturbing the frosting.

Golden Frog

AS A RULE, CLASSIC VODKA COCKTAILS WERE INTENDED TO PROVIDE AN ALCOHOLIC DRINK WITH NO TELL-TALE SIGNS ON THE BREATH AND WERE USUALLY FAIRLY SIMPLE MIXES OF NON-ALCOHOLIC FLAVOURS. CONTEMPORARY VODKA COCKTAILS OFTEN INCLUDE OTHER SPIRITS.

SERVES 1
ice cubes
1 measure vodka
1 measure Strega
1 measure Galliano
1 measure lemon juice

1 Whizz 4–6 ice cubes in a blender with the vodka, Strega, Galliano and lemon juice.
2 Blend until slushy.
3 Pour into a chilled cocktail glass.

Black Beauty

FOR A VERY DIFFERENT VERSION, TRY IT WITH ONE OF THE BLACK
VODKAS WHICH HAVE RECENTLY APPEARED ON THE MARKET. THE
DRAMATIC COLOUR AND SUBTLE FLAVOUR ARE WORTH EXPERIENCING.

SERVES 1
2 measures vodka
1 measure black Sambuca
ice
1 black olive, to decorate

1 Stir the vodka and
Sambuca with ice in
a mixing glass until
frosted.
2 Strain into an iced
cocktail glass and add
the olive.

In Vogue

Flirtini

THIS COMBINATION OF VODKA AND CHAMPAGNE IS GUARANTEED TO
BRINK A SPARKLE TO THE EYES AND A SMILE TO THE LIPS – WHAT COULD
BE MORE ATTRACTIVE?

SERVES 1
¼ slice fresh pineapple,
  chopped
½ measure chilled Cointreau
½ measure chilled vodka
1 measure chilled pineapple
  juice
chilled champagne or sparkling
  white wine

1 Put the pineapple
  and Cointreau into a
  mixing glass or jug and
  muddle with a spoon
  to crush the pineapple.
2 Add the vodka and
  pineapple juice and stir
  well, then strain into a
  glass.
3 Top up with champagne.

Vodka Espresso

THIS WOULD MAKE A FABULOUS AFTER-DINNER TREAT. IT'S USUALLY
MADE WITH STOLICHNAYA VODKA AND AMARULA, A SOUTH AFRICAN
CREAM LIQUEUR WITH A CARAMEL FLAVOUR.

SERVES 1
cracked ice
2 measures espresso or other
   strong brewed coffee,
   cooled
1 measure vodka
2 tsp caster sugar
1 measure Amarula

1 Put the cracked ice into
   a cocktail shaker, pour
   in the coffee and vodka
   and add the sugar.
2 Cover and shake
   vigorously for 10–20
   seconds, until the
   outside of the shaker is
   misted.
3 Strain into a cocktail
   glass, then float the
   Amarula on top.

Vodkatini

THE CELEBRATED 007 POPULARISED THE USE OF VODKA AS THE BASE OF
THE MARTINI, RATHER THAN GIN, HENCE THE VODKATINI IS NOW WIDELY
ACCEPTED AS AN INCREDIBLY STYLISH AND TASTY ALTERNATIVE.

SERVES 1
1 measure vodka
ice
dash dry vermouth
a single olive or a twist of
lemon peel, to decorate

1 Pour the vodka over
a handful of ice in a
mixing glass.
2 Add the vermouth, stir
well and strain into a
cocktail glass.
3 Dress with a single
olive or a twist of
lemon peel.

Flying Grasshopper

THERE ARE TWO VERSIONS OF THIS COCKTAIL – ONE MADE WITH EQUAL QUANTITIES OF WHITE AND GREEN CRÈME DE MENTHE AND ONE WITH GREEN CRÈME DE MENTHE AND CHOCOLATE LIQUEUR.

SERVES 1
cracked ice
1 measure vodka
1 measure green crème de menthe
1 measure white crème de cacao

1 Put the cracked ice into a mixing glass or jug and pour in the vodka, crème de menthe and crème de cacao.
2 Stir well and strain into a glass.

Purple Passion

THIS FRUITY COOLER STILL HAS QUITE A KICK AT ITS HEART. TRY USING ONE OF THE CITRUS-FLAVOURED VODKAS FOR A SUBTLE CHANGE IN TASTE.

SERVES 1
cracked ice
2 measures vodka
4 measure grapefruit juice
4 measures purple grape
  juice
ice cubes

1 Put the cracked ice into a cocktail shaker and pour in the vodka, grapefruit juice and grape juice.
2 Cover and shake vigorously for 10–20 seconds, until the outside of the cocktail shaker is misted.
3 Put the ice cubes into a chilled tumbler and strain the cocktail over them.

Mimi

THIS IS A DELICIOUS MIX WITHOUT THE KICK OF THE VODKA, SO MAKE A BATCH FOR NON-ALCOHOL DRINKERS AND ADD THE VODKA FOR YOURSELF!

SERVES 1
2 measures vodka
½ measure coconut cream
2 measures pineapple juice
crushed ice
slice or fan of fresh
  pineapple

1 Whizz the first four ingredients in a blender for a few seconds until frothy.
2 Pour into a chilled cocktail glass and finish with a piece of pineapple.

Metropolitan

THIS SOPHISTICATED COCKTAIL FOR CITY SLICKERS SHARES ITS NAME, BUT NOT ITS INGREDIENTS, WITH AN EQUALLY URBANE CLASSIC FROM THE PAST.

SERVES 1
1 lemon wedge
1 tbsp caster sugar
cracked ice
½ measure vodka or lemon vodka
½ measure crème de framboise or other raspberry liqueur
½ measure cranberry juice
½ measure orange juice
2 cranberries, to decorate (optional)

1 Rub the outside rim of a cocktail glass with the lemon wedge and dip it into the sugar to frost. Set aside.

2 Put the cracked ice into a cocktail shaker and pour in the vodka, liqueur, cranberry juice and orange juice.

3 Cover and shake vigorously for 10–20 seconds, until the outside of the shaker is misted.

4 Strain into the prepared glass, taking care not to disturb the frosting, and decorate with the cranberries, if you like.

Greyhound

LIKE ITS NAMESAKE, THIS IS SLEEK, ELEGANT, STYLISH AND PERFECT
FOR THE PURPOSE – IN THIS CASE A WONDERFULLY REFRESHING THIRST
QUENCHER.

SERVES 1
ice cubes
1½ measures vodka or
    lemon vodka
150 ml/5 fl oz freshly
    squeezed grapefruit juice

1 Put the ice cubes in
a highball glass and
pour in the vodka and
grapefruit juice. Stir
well.

Bullshot

THIS IS NOT UNLIKE DRINKING CHILLED CONSOMMÉ BUT WITH A KICK. IT IS BEST REALLY COLD.

SERVES 1
1 measure vodka
2 measures beef consommé
   or good stock
dash fresh lemon juice
2 dashes Worcestershire
   sauce
ice
celery salt
strip of lemon peel, to
   decorate

1 Shake all the liquid
   ingredients well with
   ice and strain into a
   medium highball glass
   with extra ice.
2 Sprinkle with celery salt
   and dress with a strip
   of lemon peel.

Chocolate Martini

FOR MANY, THIS IS THE ULTIMATE COCKTAIL. IT IS NAMED AFTER ITS INVENTOR, MARTINI DE ANNA DE TOGGIA.

SERVES 1
2 measures vodka
¼ measure crème de cacao
2 dashes orange flower water
cocoa powder, to decorate

1 Shake the vodka, crème de cacao and orange flower water over ice until really well frosted.
2 Strain into a cocktail glass rimmed with cocoa powder.

Cranberry Collins

THE CLASSIC COLLINS DRINK IS MADE WITH GIN, BUT ITS MANY
VARIATIONS ARE MADE WITH OTHER SPIRITS SO TRY THIS ONE FOR SIZE...

SERVES 1
2 measures vodka
¾ measure elderflower
  cordial
3 measures white cranberry
  and apple juice or to taste
ice
soda water
slice of lime, to decorate

1 Shake the first three
  ingredients over ice
  until well frosted.
2 Strain into a Collins
  glass with more ice and
  top up with soda to
  taste.
3 Decorate with a slice
  of lime.

Apple Martini

THE MARTINI FAMILY JUST KEEPS ON GROWING SINCE THE ORIGINAL
COCKTAIL WAS INVENTED IN NEW YORK IN ABOUT 1900 – THIS IS ONE
OF THE NEWEST AND LIVELIEST MEMBERS.

SERVES 1
cracked ice
1 measure vodka
1 measure sour apple
   schnapps
1 measure apple juice

1 Put the cracked ice
   into a cocktail shaker
   and pour in the vodka,
   schnapps and apple
   juice.
2 Cover and shake
   vigorously for 10–20
   seconds, until the
   outside of the shaker is
   misted.
3 Strain into a cocktail
   glass.

Crocodile

THIS IS CERTAINLY A SNAPPY COCKTAIL WITH A BIT OF BITE. IT PROBABLY GETS THE NAME FROM ITS SPECTACULAR COLOUR, A STARTLING SHADE OF GREEN, PROVIDED BY THE JAPANESE MELON-FLAVOURED LIQUEUR, MIDORI.

SERVES 1
2 measures vodka
1 measure Triple Sec
1 measure Midori
2 measures lemon juice
cracked ice cubes

1 Pour the vodka, Triple Sec, Midori and lemon juice over ice and shake vigorously until well frosted.
2 Strain into a chilled cocktail glass.

Silver Berry

THIS DRINK IS PERFECT FOR ONE OF THOSE VERY SPECIAL OCCASIONS – EXCEPT THAT YOU REALLY CAN'T DRINK VERY MANY!

SERVES 1

1 measure raspberry vodka, iced
1 measure crème de cassis. iced
1 measure Cointreau, iced
frozen raspberry, to decorate

1 Carefully and slowly layer the three liquors in the order listed, in a well-iced shot glass or tall thin cocktail or cocktail glass.
2 They must be well iced first and may need time to settle into their layers.
3 Decorate with a frozen raspberry.

index